A STUDENT'S GUIDE TO SCRIPTURE

CORY BROCK

SERIES EDITORS:
JOHN PERRITT
& LINDA OLIVER

paperback ISBN 978-1-5271-1283-4
ebook ISBN 978-1-5271-1308-4

10 9 8 7 6 5 4 3 2 1

First published in 2025
by
Christian Focus Publications Ltd,
Geanies House, Fearn, Ross-shire,
IV20 1TW, Great Britain
www.christianfocus.com

with

Reformed Youth Ministries,
1445 Rio Road East
Suite 201D
Charlottesville,
Virginia, 22911

Cover by MOOSE77
Printed by Gutenberg, Malta

We live in a time when "authority" is viewed with suspicion and "authoritative texts" are rejected in favor of subjective readings shaped by ideological presuppositions that resist critique. In such an atmosphere, why should anyone take the ancient message of the Bible seriously? How should we respond to its claims to speak authoritatively to all people and every aspect of human life? In this short volume, Cory Brock shows us that the Bible is unlike all other books. In it God Himself speaks to us. Through it we can know God's "personal Word"—His climactic message for the world—His Son, Jesus Christ. Cory shows us that the Bible is a trustworthy book, an internally consistent book, a thoroughly human book (it speaks in our language, to our needs), and a perfectly divine book (it's not just another record of the human quest for the spiritual. It is God talking to us, calling to us, and inviting us to know Him). Its formation, content, and character are all addressed in an accessible and compelling way. Most importantly, Cory helps us to hear the urgent call of God at the heart of the biblical message: God has acted in history, to reconcile the world to Himself through the Cross. The Bible is his invitation to us to come to know Him.

David Strain
Senior Minister, First Presbyterian Church
Jackson, Mississippi

In this short book, Cory Brock has done us all —not just students—a great favor in giving us a compelling and understandable treatment of the doctrine of God's Word. It is gracious in its tone while convincing in its message. This should be taken and given to people far and wide so that they may know how it is that we have the Bible we have, and why the Bible we have should be read and enjoyed!

Brent Corbin
Executive Director, Reformed Youth Ministries

CONTENTS

Series Introduction

Christianity is a religion of words, because our God is a God of words. He created through words, calls Himself the Living Word, and wrote a book (filled with words) to communicate to His children. In light of this, pastors and parents should take great efforts to train the next generation to be readers. *Track* is a series designed to do exactly that.

Written for students, the *Track* series addresses a host of topics in three primary areas: Doctrine, Culture, and the Christian Life. *Track's* booklets are theologically rich, yet accessible. They seek to engage and challenge the student without dumbing things down.

One definition of a track reads: *a way that has been formed by someone else's footsteps.* The goal of the *Track* series is to point us to that 'someone else'—Jesus Christ. The One who forged a track to guide His followers. While we cannot follow this track perfectly, by His grace and Spirit He calls us to strive to stay on the path. It is our prayer that this series of books would help guide Christ's Church until He returns.

In His service,

John Perritt
RYM's Director of Resources
Co-Series Editor

Linda Oliver
RYM Ministry Associate
Co-Series Editor

1. The Authority We Crave

All of us grow up and our interests change. As we get older, we tend to care about bigger questions—I'm sure you have experienced this. In 2022, Taylor Swift gave the commencement address at NYU. At one point in her speech she said, "I know it can be really overwhelming figuring out who to be ... I have some good news: It's totally up to you. I also have some terrifying news: It's totally up to you." She captured the paralysis of being a modern person. We are always being told we are our own authorities and in charge of our own identity. And that's scary. Behind her pronouncement there are so many monumental questions about our place and purpose: Who am I? What am I for? What should I do with my life? What is *my* place?

Have you asked these questions yet? Where do you get the answers? Are you supposed to look within—to your emotions and desires—

and dig deep to locate your identity and purpose? Maybe you feel exasperated by that question (how many people have asked you "what are you going to do with your life?!") and you will avoid it for a time. But eventually it may force you to ask even cosmic questions: Why is there something rather than nothing? Where did all this come from? Maybe you start to dig so deep you think about your own mind: Can I really trust that what *I* see, smell, taste, hear, and experience is actually there in front of me? How do I know that other people have minds and thoughts and an imagination like me?

The point is that the questions that matter, from the obvious, "where did this world come from," to those of identity, "who am I," to the philosophical, "do our minds conform to reality," to the practical, "who should I marry or should I get married at all," all highlight this one thing: *we are craving authority.* Is there a place I can turn to get answers? Is there authority we can trust absolutely?

In a little book on Scripture, the first thing to see is that all people need an authority for their lives—some voice that is greater than their own hearts. 1 John 3:20 should be a relief to you: "God is greater than your heart." God has given us a Word that is better than the words of our thought lives. The simple fact is that everyone is looking for *the* authority even if they don't outwardly realize or admit it. If we don't look outside ourselves for authority, it is because we believe our hearts are greater than God. All world religions—like Islam, Buddhism, and Hinduism—lean on an authoritative text, tradition, or person to find answers to the big questions. Even atheists turn to authorities. They look for the biggest names (like Richard Dawkins or Christopher Hitchens, or maybe Alex O'Connor today) and so find their authorities within this material world. Every single society that has ever existed has looked for an authority to derive their meaning, purpose, origin story, and hope, amid a bent and broken world. The question is, which authority speaks truth?

The Christian claim that has proved decisively powerful for centuries is that *God has spoken.* If God has spoken, then His Word must be the authority. If God is God, then this is a logically necessary conclusion.

For twenty-first century modern people (and especially if you've grown up around the Bible), we are not tempted so often by the religious texts of the other major world religions. Instead, the most consistently tempting message that may be pushing you away from the authority of God's Word (or may be preventing you from ever coming under God's Word) is the ever-present message of Western society: *authority is individual and personal and comes from within yourself.* In the words of 1 John, it is our natural disposition to think our hearts are greater than God. And so, our culture says, "you are your own authority." The heartbeat of our contemporary world is "be yourself," and that means "do what you want as long as you're not hurting anybody else."

We can't spend time in this little book critiquing the subjective value of modern culture. But it doesn't take much work to debunk. Consider looking at your own feelings and desires. Are you willing to say that your desires and feelings always serve you well? We want to suppress the truth about ourselves. But most people are willing to say, "there are things about me that are not good, vices and habits that I know are destructive, desires that I don't like, and patterns of thought and behavior that bring a sense of guilt and shame to my heart." As a pastor, I know that most people are aware that they aren't who they should be. It's silly to think that our feelings are superb guides for navigating reality. Don't fall into that ditch. Our desires can be terrible guides (check out Genesis 6:6-8 and Jeremiah 17:9 if you want to see what the Bible says about our hearts).

The truth is more complex. We all lean on authorities in our lives: parents, teachers, professors, scientists, mathematicians, doctors, etc. We must listen. These people are gifts to us. At the same time, none of them have all the answers; none can fix the great problems of life, not ultimately. We know that every one of these authorities are relative themselves. They are born and they pass away. They get scared. They make mistakes. They are helpful but not ultimate. We step out into the world with faith, trusting that the claims of those who came before us are often true. But we must remember that every single human is fallible. And so, we should be weary of, and protest, the loudest voice of all: our hearts—as our hearts tell us, "You are all you will ever need."

In the culture of our time, it is still true (no matter what Taylor tells you) that the *final* authority is not parents, doctors, teachers, coaches, and especially not ourselves. We may turn within, as if we're our own Scriptures, but our regular failures and confusion tell a different story. We need a voice from outside ourselves. Instead, we must see that *God has spoken.* The authorities in our lives are at their best when they believe God's Word is their ultimate authority.

What we all need is the skill of listening to that which is greater than us. We need an authority to tell us why we are (the Bible says we exist to dwell in God's presence and find joy in Him forever), what we are (the image of God, not merely a collection of atoms and quarks; you are no accident), where we are (in creation, not in a world that is a product of mere chance), and what we should do (follow Jesus the redeemer and walk in the way of the Lord; not live by the guide of our scattered feelings).

MAIN POINT:

If God has spoken, and if the Bible is God's speech, His very Word, then it must be our authority. And that means that the Bible really is the end of our search for the authority we crave.

QUESTIONS FOR REFLECTION:

- Do you believe that God has spoken? If so, why? If not, why not? Where do you turn to get answers to questions like "why is there something rather than nothing?"

- Consider how you relate to authorities in your life. If you have a big problem, where do you turn? If you have an unanswerable question, who do you talk to? Does the Bible come to mind when you are on the search for meaning?

2. That God Spoke and How God Spoke

Across the 1189 chapters and sixty-six books of the Bible, Scripture consistently says that God is invisible (see John 1:18). We know that by our own experience as well. Who has seen the Lord? God is Spirit (John 4:24). God is outside of space and time because He is "before" space and time. He made all the dimensions of creaturely reality. And that means that if you are going to know the God who made the world, God must decide to speak. God must show up. God must reveal Himself to you. And He has done it! This is called the doctrine (doctrine just means "the reality and truth") of revelation.

C.S. Lewis, in his essay "The Seeing Eye," responded to the Soviet leader Nikita Kruschev who said in 1961 that his astronauts had traveled to space but did not find God there. Lewis pointed out that going to outer space to find God would be like looking for Shakespeare within the play *Hamlet* or *Macbeth*. God is the author of this world, not a piece of the creation that you can go find. Lewis writes, "My point is that, if God does exist, He is related to the universe more as an author is related to a play than as one object in the universe is related to another."[1] Lewis is showing us that the only way to know God, the creator and author of life, is if He chooses to make Himself known. He is not one of the objects in this world you can just go and investigate, and that makes perfect sense. His revelation is necessary if we are to know God.

Holy Scripture, the Bible, is an aspect of God's revelation and a very important one. "Revelation" is not a reference to the book of Revelation written by the apostle John (though that book is part of God's revelation). The term "revelation" refers to the fact that God has revealed or unveiled Himself to us from out of His hiddenness. God, who is Spirit, full of life apart from us, absolute, perfect in being and holiness, and totally necessary, has entered space and time and shown Himself to us. This

1 C. S. Lewis, "The Seeing Eye," *Christian Reflections* (Grand Rapids: Eerdmans, 1995), pp. 167–69, 171.

is not necessary for God to do, but it is His gift to us. That is the meaning of the idea of God's "revelation." He reveals Himself in the very act of creation. He reveals Himself as creator, author, sustainer. He reveals Himself throughout world history. And then He writes about it.

If you have read the Bible, maybe you noticed the many ways God has revealed Himself: through creation (Ps. 19), through the human conscience (Rom. 2), through visions and dreams (we read about those in Scripture, like Isa. 6), through His appearance in fire and smoke (like on Mount Sinai in Exod. 3), in the glory cloud, in the tabernacle and temple of ancient Israel, through the prophets and the visitation of angels. Most of all God the Son showed up in the middle of history by taking on flesh (the incarnation). In Jesus, the invisible God has become visible. Think about Hebrews 1:1-2a: "Long ago, at many times and in many ways, God spoke to our fathers by the prophets, but in these last days he has spoken to us by his Son."

The Bible is both the gateway to God's other forms of revelation (like knowing about Jesus) and God's revelation itself. The Bible tells us about these other forms of revelation, and it also stands categorically as God's very speech. There are some who have suggested that the Bible is just God's record of revelation, an account of His speech to people a long time ago and not God's Word itself. But that is not at all what the Bible says about itself (more on that later). For us, more than anywhere else, we go to Holy Scripture to hear from God. Scripture is the most important pathway to our knowledge of God. To make a claim that big, we need to first define Scripture and then give some reasons for believing that it is God's Word.

Let's start with a definition. First, the Bible is Holy Scripture. Right. But what is Scripture? Scripture is God's speech to us through the words of human beings. Kevin Vanhoozer defines Scripture as "God's Word through the words of men."[2] Another definition we could use is that the Bible is a diverse set of books that are unified by the fact that God is the ultimate author. The Bible is divine—its original author is God. The Bible is human—it is written by many human authors. It is both. This is different than other religious texts and the claims made about them. Islamic theology says that the Koran is entirely dictated by an

2 Kevin Vanhoozer, "Holy Scripture," *Christian Dogmatics: Reformed Theology for the Church Catholic,* (Ada: Baker Academic, 2016), p. 30.

angel to Muhammad. It is not really a human text but a divinely dictated text. There is no human author, only a scribe. In Mormonism, the book of Mormon came by way of receiving divinely given golden plates, so the story goes. Most of the Hindu texts are claimed to be dictated by the gods, simply "heard" by ancient people. There are no human authors, only scribes. But Christianity makes the claim that the revelation of God written in the Bible is both God's Word and the words of human beings. We will explore this in detail later. For now, remember that the Christian view of Scripture is unique.

How do we know the Bible is what it is? Why do we look to it and say, "God has spoken"? There are many reasons. Let me offer you just a few. First, the most important thing to remember is that our lives are full of trust. We trust what other people tell us. We trust our senses. We trust that there really is good and evil and that we can tell the difference. In all this, faith stands at the beginning of all knowledge. We also come to Scripture by faith. We trust that Scripture is Scripture. Trust is such an important element of life. John Kleinig points out that just like you can only know how great good food is by eating it, so you must come to Scripture in a posture of receiving to taste and see that it is good.[3] One way to see the power of Scripture is to take up a posture of humility and to come and read the Word.

Second, while there are great, concrete reasons from outside the Bible to trust that the Bible is what is says it is, we must first listen to what the Bible says about itself. In a striking moment in 2 Peter 3, the apostle Peter mentions the letters of Paul (we have thirteen of them in the New Testament). He says this about Paul's letters: "our beloved brother Paul also wrote you according to the wisdom given him" and then Peter calls Paul's letters by the word "Scripture," which is a Greek word translated to English. The Greek word is *graphe*, which contains the idea of holy writings. The point is that Peter, who writes Scripture, says that what Paul wrote is Scripture. That means you have folks identifying the writings of the apostles as Scripture as soon as they were written. This is not some claim that came along centuries after the fact.

3 John Kleinig, *God's Word: A Guide to Holy Scripture* (Bellingham: Lexham Press, 2022), p. 1-2.

Also, consider this: if Jesus rose from the dead then you must believe everything Jesus said.[4] The resurrection vindicates His claims, His actions, His life, and His power. Jesus, we're told, went to the synagogue and opened the Old Testament and read from Isaiah in Luke 4 and He called the scroll of Isaiah "Scripture." That means Jesus Himself proclaimed the Old Testament is God's Word, or holy writing. If Jesus is who He is—the God-man, the one who died but did not stay dead—then we must believe what He believed (see Paul's argument for the centrality of the resurrection in 1 Corinthians 15).

Lastly, at the end of Luke's Gospel, in chapter 24, Jesus says that the whole Old Testament, the Law of Moses, the Psalms, and the prophets were all about Him. There we have another reason to believe the Bible is Scripture: the harmony and depth of meaning that we find woven throughout. For one example, Genesis 22 and the sacrifice of Isaac, Abraham's only beloved son, points us to an ultimate meaning in John 3:16: God called Abraham to give his only son as a sign and shadow of the fact that one day God the Father

4 For more on this, see Tim Keller's helpful arguments for believing the resurrection in his book *The Reason for God* (New York: Penguin, 2009), chapter 13.

would actually give His only Son as a sacrifice for sin. It was always about Jesus Christ. The Levitical system of sacrifices, the scapegoat released on the Day of Atonement in Leviticus 16, the high priest's role to enter the holy of holies with the blood of the lamb, these are all shadows of Christ's sacrifice for us that was to come. It is not just that they point to Jesus, but that by God's divine authorship, they were always about Jesus, even if the human author at the time could not fully see that.

To summarize, Christians call this truth (doctrine), that the Bible itself claims to be Scripture, the self-authenticating nature of Scripture. Another way to say it is that when you read what the Bible says about itself and the dimensions of connection and depth that God has offered in it, you see that the Bible vindicates itself.

You may think at first glance that this is circular reasoning. If I tell you I'm trustworthy, is it fair to say that I must be trustworthy because I said I was? Isn't that just a circular argument? Well, there are indeed lots of secondary proofs, reasons, and objective arguments for Scripture as God's Word beyond its own claims about itself. But, before you even search for them, it is so important to see that if there is a final authority that you can rely on in this life, like God's very speech, then that authority stands so far above all other authorities that you must come before it and listen, not put it to the test. You cannot put an ultimate authority under the scrutiny of judgment without trusting it first. Otherwise, you would take a lesser authority (like your very fallible mind) and use the lesser to judge the greater. There must be a rock bottom, or ultimate authority, by which everything else is known and tested. The reason you shouldn't necessarily trust someone who says "believe me, I'm very trustworthy" is because they aren't God. They may be trustworthy; they may not be. They definitely make mistakes. But if God exists, and God has spoken, we must submit to His authority rather than put it to the test.

This is what many Christians said from the earliest moments of church history. I'll just give you one example from Justin Martyr who lived from about A.D. 100–165. He writes this in his little book, *On the Resurrection*:

> *The word of truth is free, and carries its own authority, disdaining to fall under any skillful argument, or to endure the logical scrutiny*

> *of its hearers. But it [should] be believed for its own nobility, and for the confidence due to Him [God] who sends it. Now the word of truth is sent from God; wherefore the freedom claimed by the truth is not arrogant. For being sent with authority, it [is] not fit that it should be required to produce proof of what is said; since neither is there any proof beyond itself, which is God.*[5]

Before we move on, let me first invite you to go and sit and read the Bible, and to do so prayerfully, ready to receive, and in a posture that recognizes that if God exists, there must be an ultimate authority that stands above all merely human words. Consider reading some of Psalm 119, which is the longest chapter in the Bible and all about the goodness and authority of God's Word. Hear too the Word of God in the words of Jesus in Matthew 11:28, "Come to me, all you who are weary and burdened, and I will give you rest."

---

5 Justin Martyr, *On the Resurrection*, Transl. Marcus Dodds, *Ante-Nicene Fathers*, Vol. 1 (Buffalo: Christian Literature Publishing Co., 1885). Revised and edited for New Advent by Kevin Knight: www.newadvent.org/fathers/0131.html.

When you come to Scripture with a humble and repentant heart, you will find that God has spoken, and God's speech will give you rest.

MAIN POINT:

When you read what the Bible says about itself and the dimensions of connection and depth that God has offered in it, you see that the Bible vindicates itself as God's Word.

QUESTIONS FOR REFLECTION:

- Do you believe God has revealed Himself to us in this material world in which we live? Why, or why not?
- Before you read this chapter, did you already come with a posture of trust in the Bible's authority? What are some of the reasons you believe the Bible to be God's Word? Have you thought much about that question?
- How does faith and trust play a role in the other relationships of authority you have in your life?

3. What God Said

What is the message of the Bible? The Bible offers you rest. But what does that mean? 2 Timothy 3:16-17 is one of the most important passages for understanding both what the Bible is and its message. Let's think about the latter first. Paul writes this: "All Scripture is breathed out by God and profitable for teaching, for reproof, for correction, and for training in righteousness, that the man of God may be complete, equipped for every good work." We will come back to the idea of "breathed out by God" and "useful." For now, Paul tells us here that the Bible is profitable for: 1) teaching; 2) reproof and correction; and 3) training in righteousness so that we could be equipped for good works.

The first element he mentions is that the Bible is for teaching. We need to be taught. If God is God and we are creatures, it makes sense that we need to hear from God. He must tell us what it is we should know about Him and even about ourselves. Even more, if we are willing to admit that there is something lacking in us—our heart's desires are more selfish than selfless—we have to confess that we need to be told of a hope outside our own circumstances, feelings, and power to change. The concept of "teaching" here gives a sense of school-like instruction, a pronouncement, an explanation of a reality that we simply can't know on our own. The Bible teaches. But what is it that it teaches?

Well, you can open any number of pages in the Bible and find teaching. Proverbs 3:5 famously tells us to trust the Lord more than ourselves. That's wisdom. Proverbs 6:6 says to observe ants and notice their wisdom if you struggle with being lazy! Ecclesiastes tells us that the pursuit of purpose in chasing sex, money, and power is ultimately meaningless apart from hoping in God. Genesis 1 teaches us that God made the world, that it's not a product of chance—very important to recognize. Exodus 20 gives us the Ten Commandments, which have shaped Western society and remain fundamental to living the good life. You can find teaching on subjects such as sources of suffering and historical events, or learn about Hebrew poetry, Moses's style of song writing (Exod. 15), and the history of Jesus's miracles. There is much to learn.

But, amid all this teaching there is a center and a periphery. In other words, the Bible answers so many questions but there is one main message, the center. In the same way, think about the importance of your big toe. If it's broken you will struggle to walk. But your big toe is not quite as significant as your organs, especially your heart. The Bible has a heart and a big toe (so to speak), a center and a periphery. It is all God's Word and all important, *and* there is a singular message at its heart. What is the center? I like to say it like this: God knows us for who we really are and loves us anyway, enough to rescue us before we ever asked Him to.

The center of "what the Bible says" can be found in several places, but Paul makes it pretty clear in a famous passage: 1 Corinthians 15:1-4. In verse 1 he says that he wants the Corinthians to remember the "gospel" that he preached. When you look across the book of Acts, the central teaching is also what Paul calls here the gospel. Gospel comes from the Greek word *evangel* where you have a combination of a little prefix *ev* that means "good" and a word you already know: *angel.* The word *angel* doesn't just refer to one of God's heavenly hosts that comes to speak to humans on occasion. The word has a broader sense of "message." Paul says that the central teaching of Scripture is the "good message," or good news. This is not a reference to good advice but very literally to news. This is not a pronouncement of how to better yourself and get your life in gear so you can go to the best university and get a great job and be a good person. This is not a statement about being true to yourself. This is a newspaper-like announcement. This is like picking up *The Wall Street Journal* and reading the front cover headline. What is that headline?!

Paul goes on in 1 Corinthians 15:3-6, to say that the teaching of "first importance," the most important thing to know, or the "news," is this:

> *Christ died for our sins in accordance with the Scriptures, that he was buried, that he was raised on the third day in accordance with the Scriptures, and that he appeared to Cephas, then to the twelve. Then he appeared to more*

> *than five hundred brothers at one time, most of whom are still alive, though some have fallen asleep.*

Paul says the central teaching is the proclamation of a history, the history of Jesus. Jesus Christ died *for our sins*. God knew us and loved us anyway, despite our sins. God the Father sent God the Son to rescue us before we ever asked. Jesus was raised on the third day. He took up His life and claimed victory over sin and death. Jesus showed up to eyewitnesses—this happened. The gospel is the real-life history that Jesus died in your place, for the forgiveness of your guilt before God, and that His victory over sin and death in the resurrection is also your victory over sin and death. The gospel is good news, not good advice. It is the good news of grace, the unmerited favor of Jesus gifted to us. The good news is that God has reconciled us to Himself and adopted us into His family. It's all about relationship.

Back to 2 Timothy 3, the Scriptures do indeed correct us, train us in how to live, and show us that a life full of love and good works is far happier than the misery of running from God. But it does so from the resources of the gospel. The teaching of the Bible at its heart is that God rescues us *and then* shows us the way to live. That order is so important. You can't flip it around or you don't have gospel anymore. Israel had to cross through the Red Sea before they could ever hear the Ten Commandments! Salvation by grace is prior to good works.

So, the Bible's message is all about Jesus Christ. Even the Old Testament is about Jesus and the work He came to do for us, the work that only He could do. There is an incredible scene in Luke 24 that I mentioned earlier, where two of the followers of Jesus were walking to a village named Emmaus. They were chatting about all that had happened in Jerusalem. To them, Jesus had died and that very well might be the end of the story. I can't imagine what it must have been like to see the one whom you had followed, believing and wrestling with His claims to divinity, and then losing Him to Roman crucifixion and not knowing what was next. Yet, a man showed up and walked with them. They could not recognize the man—they thought Him to be a stranger.

They said to the stranger, "do you not know what happened here?!" They told the stranger that the man they thought was God's messiah, our redeemer, was murdered. But then some of the women and disciples went to His tomb on Sunday and did not find Him there! They were unsure if Jesus was dead or alive.

Then, in Luke 24:47, Luke tells us that the stranger "beginning with Moses and all the Prophets, interpreted to them in all the Scriptures the things concerning himself." This stranger was the resurrected Jesus. And He gave what must have been the greatest Bible study of all time: He went through the Old Testament and explained how the message of the Bible was always about Him and His gospel.

I hope that you are aware of the power of this proclamation. The most important sentences ever written, the most powerful words ever spoken, is the Word of the gospel. And Luke 24 says the whole Bible is about the gospel. By Jesus's real-life work God has changed the world; He has and is rescuing the world, in fact. We're told that by these words, that Jesus is Lord, at the end of human history as we know it, every knee will bow before Jesus and every tongue will confess that He is the Lord over all things, the conqueror of sin and death. One day, every person will just state the facts, but some will do so because after rejecting Jesus, they will see Him as He is, King and judge of heaven and earth.

Before we turn to see what the Bible is in more detail, let this message be for you the power that it really is. "Do not harden your heart" (Ps. 95:8) to the gospel. If the gospel is the central message of God's speech to us, then it must be the most important proclamation you will ever hear. If you confess with your mouth that what the Bible teaches at its center is true, and you believe that God raised Jesus from the dead claiming victory over your sins, you will be saved (Rom. 10:9).

Before we move on, let me give you one more way to summarize the point of the Bible. In its words, God has interpreted for us what He has done in history. The Bible is a record and song containing history and poetry, proclamation and instruction (and many different genres), of and from God's actions in this world. He created. He covenanted. He redeemed. This mighty work of God is progressive throughout history, and the Bible then progressively unfolds this history of redemption, and God Himself tells us what we should think about it (He explains it to us in His very own Words). We have in the Bible God's personal explanation of what this world is, who we are, and what He has done to save us.

For the past century or so, lots of philosophers and academics said that no one can truly interpret reality. We all come to events in our lives, world news, and any experience or circumstance, with personal baggage that forces us to see through our own subjective lenses. We see things in our own way, we're told. There is indeed some truth in this. We are fallible creatures. But what if there was a final interpretation of this world, of us, and of the meaning of history? What if God not only creates but also interprets His creation? What if God not only redeems but interprets His work of redemption, explains it to us, and even proclaims it to us?!

In Scripture, He has done it. We all need a source from which interpretation is no longer our "opinions." Remember this most important claim again: *God has spoken.*

MAIN POINT:

What is the center of the Bible's message? It is that God knows us for who we really are and loves us anyway—enough to rescue us before we ever asked Him to. The Bible is the authority that tells us that this gospel is the most important reality of human history.

QUESTIONS FOR REFLECTION:

- Can you recount the central teaching of the Bible, the gospel? What is the gospel?
- Are you compelled by the gospel? Why or why not?

4. Do We Really Have God's Word?

How do we know that the Bible we have in front of us today is the Word God intended us to have? If you turn on the History Channel or some documentary about the Bible that is made by Hollywood producers, YouTubers, or even social media influencers, you will watch the "real" story of the Bible, as they call it. It will be dramatic. There will be music and cut scenes and interviews with "scholars" with spicy takes. They will say that the New Testament was not originally intended to be written down but was an oral tradition that is unverifiable. They will claim that over the first several centuries, people started forming religious teams that stood against each other, and only then did people begin to write these books as we have them.

These docudramas will say that the twenty-seven books of the New Testament collected with the Old Testament as one book that we call the Bible is just an accident of history; there could have been more books or less. The biblical formation story in the television Bible documentary genre usually offers some narrative like this (or a similar "this is what *really* happened" story), which is there to make a point: the Bible is not God's Word, and its importance is merely a sociological circumstance.

The good news is that the best scholars don't think that. The better news is that these documentaries are more like fiction than non-fiction. Here's a bit of the history (and there is a strong consensus about it). The Old Testament was completed in the 400s B.C. at the end of the book of Malachi. Not long after that the Old Testament was recognized as a "canon," long before the time of Jesus Christ. *Canon* is a Greek word that means "measuring stick," basically. The New Testament books were written from around A.D. 40 to A.D. 90. The biblical "canon" refers to those sixty-six books that are recognized as the full measure of God's written Word—all that is included and could be included. One of the most important facts is that the New Testament books constantly quote the Old Testament and treat the Old

Testament as God's Word. The New Testament books recognize the Old Testament books as holy. No one can legitimately claim that people didn't talk about the books of the Bible as Holy Scripture until centuries later.

The four Gospels of the New Testament were all written in the first century and they were the only "gospels" written in the first century, so you can trust their proximity to the historical events. There are other so-called "gospels," like the Gospel of Thomas, which weren't written until the second century or later. That means they were definitely not written by people close to the time of Christ (because those people had all died by then). The twenty-seven books of the New Testament are all apostolic—that means either written by Apostles themselves or by someone who knew the Apostles. In the case of Hebrews, while we don't know who the author was, we see that the teaching is apostolic: it is clearly an expression of the teaching of the Apostles that fits with the rest of the New Testament. Jude 3 explains what apostolic teaching is: "Beloved, although I was very eager to write to you about our common salvation, I found it necessary to write appealing to you to contend for the faith that was once for all delivered to the saints." There was a "faith" or a set of doctrines (truths) spoken about Jesus according to the eyewitnesses and delivered to the first churches in the first century. We call that the apostolic faith. What is it? It is what we have recorded in the Bible. It is the gospel.

I hope you see that the internal evidence of the Bible won't allow such a silly claim as the TV or YouTube docudramas often make—the belief that the Bible is God's Word and that its message is true came centuries earlier. As we saw in chapter 2, Peter, from within the canon, during the very lifetime of Paul, affirms Paul's writings as Scripture from God (2 Pet. 3:16). The canon of the Bible was recognized by the earliest Christians very quickly after it was written. The message of the Bible was being spoken and tested by eyewitness, in many countries, and within a decade or two of the death and resurrection of Jesus. But most importantly, the authority of God's Bible does not find its source in human councils and decision makers from later centuries but from within itself.

What does that mean? We must see that the Word is our authority and not the other way around. The Bible is not "authorized" by an external authority like a church. Rather, the

Bible is inherently authoritative. Whether or not a church sees and says that doesn't change the fact that the Bible has authority. Even if all the churches got together and said the Bible was not authoritative, it still would be. You can't change a fact. Its authority is not based on our subjective opinions about it but on the basis that God wrote it.

In the second century, people like Irenaeus and Ignatius who were important early church fathers of the faith, were quoting from the books of the New Testament as God's Word. They did that because everyone that followed Jesus was doing that. They merely represent a preserved example of how people were treating God's Word. In the fourth century, Eusebius the historian says that the biblical books were clearly recognized as the true ones, that other books were rejected because they were not from God, and that some books were under debate. The point is, for the most part, people were able to look and tell what was from God and what was not and when it got controversial, they worked it out by the historical reception of what was already recognized.

In the same century, Athanasius lists the twenty-seven books of the New Testament canon. This is not to say that it took until then to determine the twenty-seven books. Rather, Athanasius was just an individual listing the books of the Bible as they had come to him. He was not *the guy* determining the books of the Bible, but he is a source for us. We can look at his list and realize that the Bible was already recognized as we have it. Athanasius was writing down what he had received.

It is so important to come to this issue not only with historical evidence, but also by faith with a posture of humility, approaching the Bible to be taught and shown, not to be judge and jury. In John 10:35, Jesus claims that "Scripture cannot be broken." Scripture holds up. It doesn't need us to prove it—though there are plenty of good proofs. John the apostle closes the final book of the Bible in Revelation 22:18-19 by saying that no one should add or take away from the words of this book. The prophecy is finished. The canon is closed. We have God's Word.

If someone comes to you and says, "Don't we now know that people forged these documents; that people don't really know what they actually said because they were written centuries later; weren't these books just the product of religious sects fighting each other and searching for some authority to fight some other religious group for power?" No. The historical evidence does not point in those directions. But, more importantly, because God has spoken, and because the Bible is God's Word by its own declaration, we must receive it rather than adjudicate it.[6]

MAIN POINT:

The authority of God's Word does not find its source in human councils and decision makers from later centuries but from within itself. In the printed Bibles in front of us, we really do have God's authoritative speech.

QUESTIONS FOR REFLECTION:

- How would you answer someone who comes and says that they are searching for a special, audible word from God and until they have that they won't be able to believe in Him?
- How would you address someone who is struggling with the historicity of the Bible's claims?

---

6 If you would like more on this topic, go and read Michael J. Kruger at his very helpful website that constantly explores all the questions surrounding the evidence for the Biblical canon: michaeljkruger.com.

5. The Bible Is Earthly

The Bible was written on Earth. It was not written in heaven and then dropped down on a special tablet. Most of the Bible was not dictated by God to a human being simply to be copied and passed on to us. The Bible is diverse in its genres and styles. God has chosen to speak to us in human ways through memories, records, songs, stories, parables, news, and other forms of communication because we are humans and need human forms of communication. Because the Bible records the story of redemption, which is the redemption of human beings and this creaturely world that God has made, God speaks human words to us about our human needs.

Another way to say this is that the Bible has a context(s), and that context includes specific places where humans lived: the Ancient Near East, the world of Israel, and the Greco-Roman world under the power of the Roman Empire. The Word of God comes to us in Hebrew, Aramaic, and Greek, not in a heavenly tongue with groanings that are too deep for human comprehension (Rom. 8:26). God chose to accomplish redemption and then to record that redemption in the particular cultures of Israel and the Roman empire, among others. These are not our cultures today. They are very different. God speaks His Word to us through these cultural contexts.

The most important thing to note then (and this may be a new thought for you): God chose particular human authors like Moses, David, Luke, Peter, Paul, John, Mark, James, and numerous others to speak His Words to us *using their own words* in their own contexts. While God does speak directly to many of the biblical authors and tell them exactly what to say and write, He more often uses the human authors' personal thoughts and self-selected words as His own. God does not overwhelm the human authors and treat them like machines. He wields their own thoughts and words as His very Word.

Here's an example of each. One of the most famous verses in the Old Testament is

Jeremiah 29:11, "For I know the plans I have for you, declares the LORD, plans for welfare and not for evil, to give you a future and a hope." Here, God speaks directly. He uses Jeremiah to speak His Word to the people and tells a struggling, imprisoned community in Babylon that He will rescue them. He dictates his word to Jeremiah. Think about the Ten Commandments in Exodus 20. God speaks these "ten words" directly. The Bible often records quoted speech from God—"thus says the Lord" moments.

But when you read Paul's letters (or other parts of Jeremiah, in fact) it is not direct quotation of God's voice, but Paul's own voice, or another author's own voice. Paul even says things like "imitate me!" At the same time, even in Paul's very personal words to his friends (like the greetings in his letters) we have a "thus says the Lord" text too because God speaks through Paul's own personality.

The reality that God speaks His Word through particular humans is what we call the doctrine (reality) of inspiration. Let's think about it a bit more. In 2 Timothy 3:16, Paul says that "All Scripture is breathed out by God and is profitable for teaching, for reproof, for correction, and for training in righteousness."

Notice one of the two claims we didn't explore earlier: Scripture is "beathed out by God." This is a translation of a Greek word. It looks like this in English letters: *theopneustos* (pronounce it like theo-pnoo-stos). The enormous point is that when human authors like Paul wrote letters and books that are Scripture, they did so out of their own resources as human beings in a specific culture.

Simultaneously, they did so under the power and inspiration of the Holy Spirit. The Holy Spirit did not treat them like a robot or a vehicle for dictation. He did not overpower them. When Luke or Paul write, they really do write their own words. And, as they write, the Holy Spirit guides those words, and for that reason those words are Scripture. It is not that every sentence Paul ever spoke was scriptural, not at all. Paul said things he shouldn't have sometimes just like we do. But every sentence of Paul (and all the other writers) that is recorded in the Bible is Scripture, because it is also the word of the Holy Spirit. And that means it's perfect.

There are only two things we are told were breathed out or into by God. First in Genesis 2, God breathed life into the first human. Then, in history, God breathed the Scriptures. We are full of life because the Holy Spirit continues to invigorate us (see Acts 17), and the Bible is full of life because the Holy Spirit breathed God's Word from and through the words of human beings. It's the same Spirit of God that breathes life and Scripture.

Listen to how Peter put it in 2 Peter 1:21, "For no prophecy was ever produced by the will of man, but men spoke from God as they were carried along by the Holy Spirit." Peter says that the Holy Spirit took the authors of Scripture along like a guide on a journey. The human authors used their own two legs (metaphorically), their minds, their language, their words as they wrote—and did so with God as their guide. This is a unique claim among all who have ever said they wrote holy words. God did not overtake the human authors in a trance. Of course, God could have just dropped the Bible onto Earth from heaven, but instead He chose to use the authors as partners.

This reflects how much God loves the human beings He made, and how He has always included us in a partnership with Him. Of course, God is absolute and we are relative. He doesn't need to use us. But He does. He chose specific people to be the authors of Scripture.

And while we don't have a role like that today, God continues to use us in many other ways. He has gladly allowed us to work with and for Him, and we even see that in the Holy Spirit's work of inspiration through the human authorship of the Bible.

MAIN POINT:

The Bible is not dropped out of the sky from heaven to Earth. Instead, the Holy Spirit took the authors of Scripture along like a guide on a journey. God used their minds, culture, and words to write His Word.

QUESTIONS FOR REFLECTION:

- How do you think God's use of particular people and contexts matters for how we read and interpret the Bible today?
- If you think about the lives and biographies of some of the authors of Scripture (David and Paul for example), what does that tell you about God's disposition toward humanity?

6. The Bible Is Heavenly

The Bible is multi-authored. There are many human authors (and some of them we do not know by name), but there is one divine author. God is the ultimate author of the Bible. Now, let's think about the implications that the Bible is not only earthly but also "heavenly," written by God Himself. Let me give you seven (it just worked out that way).

First, it makes sense that God has given us written words as a text to live by because of what He reveals about His own use of words from the beginning of history. God is the maker of heaven and earth and one of the first things we learn about God when He creates is that He is a speaker (Gen. 1). He uses words to create heaven and earth. God uses language. As God's image, we are speakers too and we use the gift of language in a human way that reflects God's divine speech. God speaks words in a way we cannot even understand, but tells us that our language reflects His language. The point here is this: If God has been speaking words to us from the beginning of time, even using words to create the world, it makes sense that He would speak to us now by a word.

Second, Scripture is a unified collection of diverse writings, and the unity of the Bible is grounded in God's authorship. Where could unity come from when you have sixty-six books that span thousands of years? Only from God as author. If God is the ultimate author, then we can collect books that do span thousands of years, and books from many different contexts containing many different genres, and we can call it one book. It is one book because God wrote it. And because God transcends space and time, He can use enormous spans of time to write one book with as many authors as He chooses.

Third, the other element I mentioned in the previous chapter from 2 Timothy 3 is that Paul says that Scripture is "profitable" beyond its immediate context. The immediate context includes the first people that each book of the Bible was written to. But the Bible is powerful beyond that context, reaching even into our own context. This is an enormous claim. The idea of the writings of human beings having power beyond their immediate moment suggests that these actually are God's words that have authority and power across every age. The Bible can only be powerful to us if it is indeed God's very Word.

Fourth, when you think about both the idea of Scripture "breathed out by God" and the fact that the Bible is written by specific human authors in a Jewish and Greek and Roman and Ancient Near Eastern context, you realize that we must both read the Bible in its original context and also ask how it impacts our context, because God wrote it to them and to us. Kevin Vanhoozer suggests that because the Bible was written on Earth, we have to think about its many contexts on Earth in order to read it rightly.[7] That means that to understand the Bible we must first ask, "What did God say to the first audience," and through that message we then ask, "What then is God saying to us today?" Because we are reading God's Words, they are "profitable" and powerful for us today. It is not despite these many contexts but through them that we

7 Vanhoozer, "Holy Scripture," p. 30–56.

are able to approach Scripture as a mirror by which we see ourselves for who we really are. God speaks truth to *us* through these particular people and their words.

Fifth, think for a moment about the implications that God chose to write a book for us. Oral tradition is not nearly as durable as the written text. Oral traditions are powerful, and God has used people to tell of His works from generation to generation. But a written word really lasts. That means God, as ultimate author of Scripture, has protected His Word for century after century. We have manuscripts on top of manuscripts of the Bible. Through writing, God consistently gives human records of His mighty works. The Holy Spirit preserves the Bible for us and that history is like a divine stamp of approval on the Bible.

Sixth, since this written text from God is useful beyond the moment it was written, that means it is the book for all of God's people. The Bible is God's Word; it gathered and still gathers people in every nation and every century from every tribe and tongue. We couldn't possibly count how many people God has changed through His Word. But we can talk about this reality, that God has used His Word to gather one people across a diversity of lands and times, with one very important word: "catholic." The word "catholic" does not refer to the Roman Catholic Church, but to the universal character of God's people. "Catholic" means universal. So right now, in this very moment, you can know that when you read God's Word and you submit to God's voice, you are doing so with millions and millions and millions who live in other parts of the world and who lived in other centuries as one people. This includes a unity we really do have with the historical characters the Bible talks about. You get to hear God's voice in His Word just like your brother in Christ, Isaiah, or your sister in Christ, Ruth!

Seventh, and very importantly, because the Bible is God's Word, heavenly speech, it is pure (Ps. 19:8). In a way that is analogous to the incarnation (that the Son of God became human), Scripture can be "human" and remain pure, or without error. Jesus is both human and divine. Jesus is the God-man and He is sinless. Of course, Scripture is not God. Scripture is not Jesus. But it is both a human and divine word and because it is a divine word, it is pure. God's Word is truth (Ps. 19:9) because God speaks truth. There are a couple of important implications here.

First, the text itself is authoritative. The power of Scripture is not just in our experience. Lots of people have said that when we read the Bible, we read a record of God's Word to other people. It is not really God's Word to us, but just to them in their time. No. That is not what the Bible claims about itself. It is not just a historical document where you can have an engaging emotional experience, it is the objective truth and authority because it is God's very speech.

Second, if the Bible is God's Word because God is the ultimate author, we must see that the Bible is infallible. If it is infallible, that means it is without error, or inerrant. This means that all God desires to do when He speaks, He does. He doesn't make mistakes and neither does His Word.

As we conclude this chapter, let me answer a question that often comes up after considering that the Bible is God's authoritative Word to us: If the Bible is infallible truth based upon God's infallible speech, then is the Bible all we need to know about everything? Can you turn to the Bible to learn about geology, sociology, geography, mathematics, and other similar subjects? Should you?

There is a sense in which the answer here is "yes," but it should be obvious that the answer is "no." We don't open the Bible to learn calculus or about contemporary political battles between nation-states. It is not true to suggest that all knowledge about this world and us is found in Scripture. We also have what has been called the "book of nature." Our minds are always working rapidly to see and perceive all that God has made in its array of forms, like numbers in mathematics, rocks in geology, and relationships in sociology.

And, at the same time, we can also say "yes" because the Bible provides the system by which we understand mathematics, geology, and sociology, and all the other areas of study. For example, you can study geology all you want but you will never find within geology an answer to the question "where did the rocks first come from and what are they ultimately for?" You can study sociology and consider the dynamics of the entertainment industry, for example, but never arrive at a solution to fundamental questions: What are people ultimately looking for when we they seek entertainment? What does the allure of celebrity always prove empty? Why are we addicted to entertaining ourselves? The more we investigate this world, the more we bump into questions that don't have answers from within this world. The Bible declares that God is the maker of heaven and earth, all things visible and invisible. Colossians 2:3 makes an enormous claim that in Jesus Christ "are hidden all the treasures of wisdom and knowledge." Ultimately, God is the reason that all the arenas of study and knowledge in our lives exist. He made everything. The point of everything that exists is to serve His glory and our joy in His presence. And so, while the Bible doesn't teach you calculus, it tells you where calculus comes from and why you can trust that mathematical axioms don't change—because you have a consistent God who created them and maintains all things, including numbers.

Here's one last example. We can study history, but if we try and assess history with words like "good" and "evil," how can we say that we know for sure who the good guys and bad guys were? If two countries are at war, and the first country says, "We are the good guys" and then the second country says "No, they are evil. We are the good guys," who gets to decide the truth? God does. The Bible offers a clear, persuasive account of the reality of morality. It tells us what is good and what is valuable. It tells us what is evil and destructive. Think about it. If ethics is relative to culture, where could we turn to finally determine what is just and unjust? This can even happen within a family. You can have two or three different opinions on whether it was right or wrong to move house, to marry that person, to take that job. How do we know? We need a final authority. God, the author of Scripture, has spoken.

MAIN POINT:

Because God is the author of Scripture, everything God intends to do when He gives us each sentence in the Bible, He does. He speaks authoritatively, without error, and therefore purely.

QUESTIONS FOR REFLECTION:

- If a friend challenges your faith in God's Word by saying that the Bible is full of errors and contradictions, what would you say? What are some steps for helping a friend see that the Bible is without error?
- Can you think of some other examples of how the Bible helps you to understand some of the subjects you study?

7. The Bible Is Light

I remember growing up in a church in south Mississippi where we did a lot of singing—kid's choirs, stuff like that. As kids, we would always sing a song by Amy Grant (and the tune is in my head as I write this) with these lyrics: "Thy word is a lamp unto my feet and a light unto my path … when I am afraid, think I've lost my way, still you're there right beside me." We teach songs like this to kids so that one day they will do what I've just done: remember it. I remembered it in my university years realizing for the first time that the Bible was serious and that lines like the ones I grew up singing weren't just for the sake of providing a kids program. God had to let me run away a bit before I saw the power of His Word. The Holy Spirit came and convicted me, changed me, pardoned me, and set me on the path I walk today, through the power of the Word of God. It took me a number of years to see that the Bible was to be taken seriously, that it had power.

The Amy Grant song is a quote, as you may know, from Psalm 119:105, "Your word is a lamp to my feet and a light to my path." God's Word is light. It has a luminosity about it that shines out when you're awake to see it and it shines straight through the heart, exposing and remaking. Light is an important metaphor in Scripture. In the light of Christ, we see light: "Jesus Christ is the way, the truth, and the life. No one comes to the Father except by Him" (John 14:6). Jesus was the light that knocked Paul off his horse on the road to Damascus, blinded him, and then set him free from his legalism (Acts 9). This little chapter is about application. Here are three ways the Bible is light to you (and I hope you'll be knocked over by God's Word):

1) The Bible is the only light we really need
2) The Bible is light enough for what we need to know
3) The Holy Spirit brings light as we read it.

First, think again about Psalm 119:105, "Your word is a lamp to my feet and a light to my path." The Bible is the lamp that lights the pathway to salvation. It tells you how to get to Jesus and it does a good job of it! Light brings clarity. As soon as you walk into a dark room and flip the light on, there is an instant transfer from a sense of being lost to the glory of sight. The Bible is the switch that brings clarity into our lives regarding the kind of rescue we need. The Bible is clear in telling us who we are, what's wrong with us, what we were made for, and how to find the hope of salvation. Put simply, the Bible is clear on what we need it to tell us.

But you may say "not always to me!" What do we mean by the statement: "The Bible is clear"? When Jesus is talking to the Pharisees and the crowd in Matthew 12:3, 5, and 19:4, He asks, "Have you not read?" What does He mean? He means that if you read the Old Testament, you should have understood it. You should have seen. The religious leaders didn't see because they didn't want to see. Their hearts were hard to the convicting message that Jesus was speaking from the Old Testament. Jesus was making the point that people don't need master's degrees from Ivy League universities to understand the point of Scripture. It is all about Him. It is all about Christ our light, and the light that Scripture provides makes our groping in the dark for salvation and rescue a distant memory.

The Westminster Confession of Faith in chapter 1, paragraph 7, reminds us of something very helpful: Not everything in Scripture is equally easy to understand. If you've read Ezekiel, you know that it's harder than John 3:16. Remember that even Peter says sometimes Paul's writings are hard to understand (2 Pet. 3:16). *And* remember John 3:16, "For God so loved the world, that he gave his only Son, that whoever believes in him should not perish but have eternal life!" That sentence is pretty clear. The Westminster Confession goes on to say that while sometimes the Bible requires some work to hear what God is saying, the central message of the Bible is clear for all, no matter how much education a person may or may not have. What is to be believed for salvation—that is what is clear! Confess with your mouth that Jesus is Lord and believe in your heart that God raised him from the dead (Rom. 10:9). The Bible brings the light of salvation to you—it tells you that Jesus is the way.

Second, there's another aspect of the light of the Bible: Scripture is light enough for our path. It is *enough* to light the way for our lives until we see Jesus. There is a consistent desire in our hearts: we want to hear from God and we want to see God. Once you've experienced the grace and presence of God, you want more and more of the things of God. Remember how Moses said, "Can I see your glory" (Exod. 33:18)? These are good desires, to want more of God. But, sometimes, that good desire becomes a bit muddied, and we start to think and say implicitly (or even explicitly): "If God would show Himself to me, if God would speak a clear, audible word to me, then I could really believe." And so, we go searching and searching for God's speech in all sorts of ways. And it is totally true that God speaks today. God gives us desires and inclinations, and He uses people to impart wisdom. God shows us pathways in our lives by way of personal peace, and through the opportunities He opens and closes. But we need to remember that God has spoken decisively in Scripture.

Think about the story that Jesus told about the rich man and Lazarus in Luke 16:19-31. The rich man was condemned for being addicted to his money. He had literally lost his name and had become nothing more than "rich man." He loved money so much it became his idol. But now, in judgment, the rich man longed for the opportunity to go and speak to his relatives and warn them about the doom that worshiping money brings. And Jesus says that even if the rich man rose from the dead and spoke to his relatives it wouldn't matter since they weren't listening to "Moses and the Prophets" (v.31). That means that Jesus was convinced that the Bible is enough for us. We must listen to it and not look for more. And yet, the reason we feel that inclination for more is because we have deep desires to see God and to hear God. The Bible is enough for now. Read and pray. But we do both awaiting the day where we will "see him as he is" (1 John 3:2). Our longings for more are right, but our search for more than God's written Word right now is often misguided. God's Word is sufficient for what we need. God knows what He is doing. The Bible really is light enough.

Third, the Bible is for you. The Holy Spirit speaks today and brings light to our lives, but He does so in a particular way. There was an age of inspiration (God-breathed through the authors of Scripture), but now we live in an age of illumination (God the Spirit opens our eyes to see the truth of His Word). God has extended His power unto us by sending His Word and His Spirit together. Paul talks about this in 1 Corinthians 2:14 when he says that the things of God are "spiritually discerned." That means that reading the Bible and believing in Jesus is not just about getting your head right. It is not a logical movement to a proven conclusion. Rather, it requires an act of the Holy Spirit to change our hearts from hard to soft, from angry at God to grateful to God, from darkness to light. We need light. We need to be illumined by the presence of God the Spirit to hear God's Word. The Bible is not only God-breathed but God-breathing. God continues to speak to you in His Word. He both inspired His Word and continues to illumine His Word to us.

What can you do today? Depend on Scripture. Are you aware of your need to hear God's word? The Bible is the rule of faith and life—that means that the Bible is the place to go to understand what you need to be saved from and how you should live in light of this salvation. Sometimes, you may not feel the power of God's Word when you read it. That does not mean it is not powerful. Our emotions are not the final arbiter of truth. Often, we need to come to the Bible over and over for our feelings to follow the good of our actions and habits.

All this means that the Bible is integral to your discipleship. It would be very hard to grow closer in relationship to Jesus Christ without taking seriously the Word that Jesus said is God's Scripture to us. It is a means of grace to us. That means that when you read the Bible, even if your feelings aren't working too strongly at one moment, God speaks. God the Holy Spirit is present, and the Word does not leave you unchanged. Sometimes when we come to Scripture with a hard, angry, bitter heart, the Word of the Bible can discipline us, convict us, and show us the way home. Sometimes when we come with a hard heart, our hearts can get harder! We can get angry and refuse to hear God's voice. That is why the writer to the Hebrews says, "Do not harden your heart" (Heb. 3:15). Come with a posture ready to be broken and re-made by Scripture. The Bible in this way becomes a mirror by which we see who we really are, a window by which we see who we should be like (Jesus!), and a doorway by which we can come to the one who can pardon and renew. Sing Scripture. Pray Scripture. Speak the Words of Scripture to others. Hear Scripture preached. Hear it read! Read it! Take up and read.

MAIN POINT:

The Bible is the light we need in our lives. It offers a clear message of salvation (clarity). It is light enough for the path we walk in this life until we see Jesus (sufficiency). The Holy Spirit brings light to our hearts as we read it (illumination).

QUESTIONS FOR REFLECTION:

- Do you have a habit of reading the Bible? What are some ways you could change your schedule to make time for reading Scripture? What in your life do you need to drop to be able to have the time for what's most important?
- Do you have a story of how the Bible has impacted you? Can you share a moment where the God used His Word in a powerful way in your life?

8. The Word, the Word, and the Word Himself

The Bible tells us that Jesus is the Word made flesh (John 1:14). Perhaps you've noticed that we call Jesus the Word and at the same time we call Scripture the Word. They are obviously not the same. Jesus is the Son of God and a true human being. He was a carpenter, and He had siblings; He is the flesh and blood Messiah. He was born of Mary, conceived by the Holy Spirit. Jesus is very God of very God, as one of our old church creeds tells us.

Scripture is a book. It is written and printed. It is not God Himself. And yet we use the term "Word" for both the Word of the Lord as Scripture and the Word Himself, Jesus. Let me throw a wrinkle in here to add that when Paul and Barnabas are preaching on their missionary journey, we are told by Luke, the writer of Acts, that the newly converted Christians "[glorified] the word of the Lord" (Acts 13:48) and the Word "continued to increase and prevail mightily" (Acts 19:20). Here, the term "Word" is referencing apostolic preaching. Heinrich Bullinger, one of the Reformers, said that even preaching is the Word of God.

What do we do with these three references to the Word of the Lord? We confess that the Bible teaches a *three-fold form of the Word of God*. That means that there are three distinct yet connected forms in which God speaks His Word to us. Obviously, the Bible is not Jesus. And even more obviously, your preacher's preaching is not Jesus. And yet when the Bible is read, we are reading God's Word, and when the preacher preaches the gospel, we are hearing God's Word. Every preacher you listen to can also sometimes preach his own words that are in no way the Word of God. Preaching is only God's Word if the preacher preaches God's Word, and specifically preaches the personal Word Himself, Jesus Christ.

The three-fold form of the Word of God is all connected by Jesus himself. Jesus is the Son of God who spoke from creation. Colossians 1:17 says His words uphold the world at this very moment. He is the main content of God's speech. Jesus is the speech that God wants us to hear. And so, Jesus is the main content of the Bible. Jesus is the center of the Bible's message, the center of good preaching, and the personal Word Himself, very much God! So, if Jesus says the Bible is God's Word, then the Bible is God's Word. And if the Bible says that preaching is God's Word, then it is. It is Jesus, the personal Word, that ultimately gives power to the Word of God as Scripture and the Word preached.

The three-fold form of the Word helps us to see that Jesus is the only Word we worship. Jesus is the personal Word, the *logos* of God, as John puts it in John 1:1. The Bible is not the "personal" Word, because the Bible is not a person. So we worship Jesus, not the Bible. But we come to the Bible and know it is indeed God's Word and the pathway for us to know Jesus. While the Word of God in Scripture is not the Word Himself—and so we must beware of bibliolatry, where we come to worship the text and not the ultimate author—we must also beware of the ditch of downplaying the power and importance of Scripture by saying, "All we need is Jesus," not the Bible. Neither denying the power of God's Word in Scripture to make more of Jesus, nor treating the Bible like God

Himself and thereby making less of Jesus, are the paths of light. Instead, Jesus is the Word of God as God Himself, our savior. And Scripture is the speech of God that brings us to the Word Himself. We need the latter to have the former.

Another way to say this is that the Bible is the servant form of God's Word. It is there to tell us about the God we worship. It serves God's ultimate purpose that every knee would bow to the Word Himself, Jesus, by teaching us about the Word Himself. God gave it to us as His Word so that we might glorify God by seeing the power of the Word of the cross—Jesus's death in our place. I like how A.W. Tozer puts it:

> *"The Bible is not an end in itself, but a means to bring people to an intimate and satisfying knowledge of God, that they may enter into Him, that they may delight in His Presence, may taste and know the inner sweetness of the very God Himself in the core and center of their hearts."*[8]

This also helps us to see that we must take the preaching of God's Word at church seriously.

8 A.W. Tozer, *The Pursuit of God* (Chicago: Moody Publishers, 2015), p. 10.

When we hear God's Word preached, we hear God's Word. Here is what Bullinger wrote in the Second Helvetic Confession in 1566: "When this Word of God is now preached in the church by preachers lawfully called, we believe that the very word of God is preached and received by the faithful." So, Bullinger said that when the Bible is proclaimed, and particularly the saving message of the gospel, by preachers who have been tested and approved by the church to teach, God's Word goes forth to human beings. Bullinger did not make this up. He got it from the Bible. When the first Christians preached the word of the gospel in their own words, the Bible said people received it as God's Word (1 Thess. 2:13). This mean that we believe that God is still working through the Word of the gospel proclaimed.

The Holy Spirit who breathed out Scripture is the same Holy Spirit who moves through the preaching of Scripture to bring power to the hearers. This Holy Spirit is the one who also illumines our hearts to see Scripture's truth and brings light to our darkened hearts. And this is the very Spirit who points us to the Word Himself, Jesus, and applies the work of Jesus to us in salvation. You can see the close connection between the Spirit and the Word. When God speaks, by the presence of the Holy Spirit, He brings power and fulfills His pronouncement in Isaiah 46:11, "I have spoken, and I will bring it to pass; I have purposed, and I will do it." God always does what He intends to do. His Word always goes forth in power.

MAIN POINT:

The three-fold form of the Word of God is all connected by Jesus Himself. He is the main content of God's speech. Jesus is the center of the Bible's message, the center of good preaching, and the personal Word Himself, very much God!

QUESTIONS FOR REFLECTION:

- Have you ever considered preaching to be the Word of God? How does that change the way you approach listening to a sermon when it is given from the Bible?
- Can you describe in your own words the connections between the Holy Spirit and the three-fold form of God's Word (Jesus, the Bible, Preaching)?

9. Never Hide from Hard Questions

We have been considering the doctrine of Scripture. The Bible is Holy; it is Scripture. It is holy because God is the ultimate author of Scripture. The Bible is God's Word through the words of human beings. But, as you probably know very well, many modern people do not believe this. The skeptic says the Bible is an interesting historical artifact that has been useful for some societies but is now antiquated and surpassed by science. The average person, the populous, just gets on with their lives seemingly indifferent—never really thinking too much about where this world comes from and whether there could be a Word of the Lord to hear. More suspicious people say that the Bible is good to a degree, Jesus is a moral example perhaps, but they can't get behind the text in order to verify the historical scenes they read about.

Others take a more economic route: Why take the time to study the nature of Scripture? Why even take time to read the Bible? In this twenty-first century life, time is money, after all! We are busy people. We have voices coming at us all the time. But what if there *was* a Word from God? What if the One who is from before space and time spoke to you? If that was the case, you would have to say there is one place to go and find answers; there is one Word that is above and better than all others. In the Bible, that's what we have.

These different forms of pushback have been around for centuries. But the Bible ultimately explains why people (including us) often can respond to the Bible in these ways: because we have rejected the God who made us, and our hearts are turned against God's speech. Another way to say it is that we are not sinners because we sin, but we sin because we are sinners. From the beginning of our lives, we are in a struggle as sinners against God and His Word. I have been suggesting with the church of old that we desperately need to take up a posture of trust and humility in this life, before God and before His Word. There are many good reasons for believing the historical truths of Scripture, such as the consistency of the manuscript tradition that has brought the Bible to us today. These are big helps to our faith. But we must realize that there comes a point where we must decide to trust in the Word of God because God is greater than our hearts. My appeal to you is to come and read the Word of God open to this claim, that the Bible is God's Word, with true humility—not seeking to be a judge of God's Word but to be judged and uplifted by it.

So, the most important thing this book can do is convince you that the Bible is the Word of God and send you on your way to reading Scripture. If you've grown up in the church, that may sound old hat to you. But let me ask you to rethink the weightiness of the claim of this little book: In the Bible, God has spoken! In the eighteenth century, a series of what we call "revolutions" took place, and from there a culture that once submitted to God's Word became the cultures we know today: in many places, the Bible has no role in the lives of most people.

A significant turn away from Scripture happened around the time of the French Revolution. In 1789 in Notre Dame, that famous Parisian

Cathedral was transformed into a "temple of reason," which was a way of denying the authority of the Bible and pronouncing that modern people were too smart for their predecessors. Even now, we worship "freedom and equality," the two great ideals of the French Revolution. "We now know by means of our own research," so the narrative went. We can put everything we know into the encyclopedia (or Wikipedia). And with the rise of A.I., the French revolutionaries would be ecstatic: finally, there is something that can understand everything. (In truth, my experience with A.I. is that it is very bad at understanding lots of things, especially theology!). The point is that for the last 250 years or so, modern people have replaced external authority with internal authority. The more we know, the more we will be free. We have located the authority we crave—within. For a while, our craving was focused on knowledge accumulation, and now it is focused on feeling and desire.

But if you read the Bible, you will see that this is exactly what happened in the Garden of Eden in Genesis 3. The Serpent tempted Eve by saying, "Don't you want to be like God?" The first and great temptation, which took us away from the safety of submission in Eden to the danger of independence in exile, was through the question, "Did God really say?" In other words, "Don't you know, human being, that if you stop listening to God's Word and you take a stand and listen to your feelings you will become as great as God is?" Essentially, Satan said that if you want to be like God, as powerful as God, trust your heart to guide you. Do not listen to God's Word. Yet the denial of God's Word brought this world into death and chaos.

No singular proof for the truthfulness of God's Word can ever be the "One Thing" that brings us from skepticism to faith. Though God can use proofs powerfully, we need to see that our hearts were persuaded from birth by the question "did God really say?" that Satan spoke at the beginning of history. We want to be our own gods. Our hearts must be overcome by the God who is greater than our hearts. We must see that we want to be our own authority. We must be honest in order to come to a place where we can confess our need for a better authority.

Let's conclude with this. I hope and pray that you are walking with God and listening to God speak through His Word. But, if you are, you will likely hear questions from those that are not, and you will likely have questions arise in your own heart about what to do with some of the more difficult moments to understand. What do you do when you are asked hard questions about Scripture? What do you do when you talk with someone who is in search of the truth, but not yet able to see the power of God's Word? What about some of the laws in the Old Testament that seem so strange? What about the conquest of holy war that God's people enacted in the book of Joshua? What about the four Gospels and their seemingly different timelines? Here are five rules to remember going forward:

First, never hide from these questions. You don't need to. All of these and many more have been well-answered throughout church history. There are no new questions or new doubts. God's people have received them all and carefully thought through them.

Second, steel-man everyone's arguments against the Bible. That means don't try and undercut other people by offering an easy-to-knock-down version of their reasons for being a skeptic. Instead, attempt to understand their point of view better than even they can. That will show how much you care.

Third, go and read the resources that are available on the questions and arguments being considered from the best possible sources that you are able to read. There are great answers and helpful considerations from so many people in so many places and centuries, but you do need to do the work of finding and considering the answers. Remember, 1 Peter 3:15 gives us a very important command: always be ready to give a reason for what you believe to anyone that asks you.

Fourth, listen to the last bit of that verse I just quoted: always be ready to give a reason for what you believe, "yet do it with gentleness and respect." Your goal is not to win arguments for the Bible but to see people changed by the very real gospel that God has spoken in the Bible. Your first commitment in approaching people who have questions is to love them.

Fifth, bring your personal doubts to God and to wise Christians that will let you work them out. In Jude 22, through Jesus's brother, God says to "have mercy on those who doubt." God does. He did for Thomas. He did for Moses. Take your questions to God in prayer.

MAIN POINT:

Never hide from hard questions about the Bible. Take your questions and doubts to God in prayer and seek the help of so many who have come before you and thought carefully through such questions.

QUESTIONS FOR REFLECTION:

- What are some of the questions that have come up for you when reading the Bible? Can you think of specific passages or stories? Who do you have in your life that you can discuss these questions with? Are you making use of them?
- Have you ever fielded questions from others about the Bible? Reread 1 Peter 3:15 and discuss what it means for talking to those who have yet to believe the power of God's Word.

Epilogue: What it Took to Get an English Bible

In chapter 7, I wrote about several ways that the Bible is light for your path. The Bible is indeed for you. This means that you should be able to read it in your language, just as you are reading this sentence right now. Thankfully, there are about 900 translations of the Bible today in the English language. We assume there is always a Bible nearby for us to read. And we take for granted the immense gift it is to own a copy of the Bible (or ten!) and to read it in our language. It's so normal we don't even think about it. Do you know the stories of sacrifice behind the English Bible? Let me offer you one as we conclude this book. I hope this story will help you to cherish the book you hold in your hands the next time you pick up a printed English Bible.

William Tyndale provided the first English Bible translated from Hebrew and Greek. He was able to translate the New Testament and parts of the Old Testament before his death. Tyndale was born in the 1490s and he lived during a time when the Roman Catholic Church didn't want the Bible to be translated. They preferred the Bible to stay in Latin, which was the translation they had been using for many centuries. Tyndale went to Oxford and Cambridge. He was very smart! He was a gifted linguist and knew a lot of languages. He made it his life goal to translate the Bible because he wanted to give the Bible to all who spoke his language, English. It's hard to imagine a time where you could not read the Bible unless you knew Latin. The Bible was restricted to very few people. Tyndale wanted to give the gift of Scripture to all. A century before, the Roman Catholic Church had decided (in parts of Europe) that translating the Bible was a heretical act—meaning that anyone convicted of translating the Bible would be considered a criminal act and killed (and that happened on several occasions in the 1400s).

Tyndale began translating the Bible into English in the 1520s. He had to flee England to get the work done. He went to Cologne, Germany and finished the Bible translation in 1524. The English Bible was printed and imported into England in all sorts of secret ways, especially by hiding them in German merchant ships. The bishops of the Roman church throughout England called this work "heresy" and would burn all copies they could find. For them, heresy meant that you had condemned yourself before God and the government and so you deserved death both in this life and the next. For translating the Bible, the bishops said Tyndale deserved to die. One bishop in particular, Thomas More, did everything he could to hunt down Tyndale. He used spies, and he even broke the law to catch Tyndale. Thomas More killed six of Tyndale's friends and supporters for promoting the English Bible.

Tyndale came back to England from Belgium in the 1530s and was betrayed and given over to the authorities. He was imprisoned in 1536, condemned, and was tortured and executed in October, all for translating the Bible into English. At the moment of his death, he cried out, "Lord, open the eyes of the King of England."

Let us not take the English Bible for granted. We do not often appreciate the cost that was paid so we could be lavished in printed English Bibles. Take up and read.

Appendix A: Next Steps

What can we do now?

PRAY

Here is a prayer that you can use as you approach the Bible: Our Father, I know that I do not live by bread alone but by every word that comes from your mouth. Make me hungry for this food that you offer in Scripture and help me to receive it. Give me understanding and give me desire for you and for every word you speak, so that I can be nourished by your Word. In Jesus's name I ask this, Amen.

READ

Now, go and read Scripture! There are lots of good options out there for working your way through the Bible. There are many different approaches. My suggestion to you is to read a Psalm or two every day and use them as prayers. Then read through a book of the Old Testament and New Testament slowly, little by little, each day. Meditate on the words and pray them back to God as you read them.

ATTEND

Next, go and renew your approach to hearing God's Word preached. Read the passage that the preacher is preaching on before you go to church. Reflect on it. Pray beforehand that God would open the eyes of your heart. Listen with intent.

SHARE

Focus on 1 Peter 3:15 for a season, and read another book or two that may help you answer questions about the Bible. Always be prepared to give an answer for the hope that is within you!

Appendix B: Other Books on this Topic

Colin J. Fast, *A Student's Guide to Reading and Applying the Bible*, Track: Christian Life (Fearn: Christian Focus, 2025).

Kevin DeYoung, *Taking God At His Word* (Wheaton: Crossway, 2014).

David Daniel, *William Tyndale: A Biography* (Yale: Yale University Press, 1994).

John Kleinig, *God's Word: A Guide to Holy Scripture* (Bellingham: Lexham Press, 2022).

Get the whole set of *Track* books:

Doctrine:
A Student's Guide to...

- *Apologetics*
- *Living Out Reformed Theology*
- *Justification*
- *Sanctification*
- *Glorification*
- *Missions*
- *Scripture*
- *Church*

Culture:
A Student's Guide to...

- *The Power of Story*
- *Navigating Culture*
- *Worldview*
- *Technology*
- *Social Media*
- *Gaming*
- *Politics*

Visit
christianfocus.com

Christian Life:
A Student's Guide to...

- *Reading and Applying the Bible*
- *Grief*
- *Body Image*
- *Purity in a Porn-Satured Culture*
- *Depression*
- *Anxiety*
- *Dating, Marriage, and Sex*
- *Womanhood*
- *Rest*

Reformed Youth Ministries (RYM) exists to serve the Church in reaching and equipping youth for Christ. Over the last five decades RYM has grown from a single summer conference into three areas of ministry:

- **Conferences:** RYM hosts multiple summer conferences for local church groups in a variety of locations across the United States.
- **Training:** Youth Leader Training (YLT) is for anyone serving with youth in the local church. RYM also offers a Church Internship Program in partnering local churches, youth leader coaching, and youth ministry consulting services.
- **Resources:** RYM offers a growing array of resources for leaders, parents, and students.

RYM is a 501(c)(3) non-profit organization. To learn more or to partner with RYM in reaching and equipping the next generation for Christ please visit rym.org.

Christian Focus Publications

Our mission statement

Staying Faithful

In dependence upon God we seek to impact the world through literature faithful to His infallible Word, the Bible. Our aim is to ensure that the Lord Jesus Christ is presented as the only hope to obtain forgiveness of sin, live a useful life and look forward to heaven with Him.

Our Books are published in four imprints:

CHRISTIAN FOCUS

Popular works including biographies, commentaries, basic doctrine and Christian living.

MENTOR

Books written at a level suitable for Bible College and seminary students, pastors, and other serious readers. The imprint includes commentaries, doctrinal studies, examination of current issues and church history.

CHRISTIAN HERITAGE

Books representing some of the best material from the rich heritage of the church.

CF4KIDS

Children's books for quality Bible teaching and for all age groups: Sunday school curriculum, puzzle and activity books; personal and family devotional titles, biographies and inspirational stories – because you are never too young to know Jesus!

Christian Focus Publications Ltd,
Geanies House, Fearn, Ross-shire,
IV20 1TW, Scotland, United Kingdom.
www.christianfocus.com